The Essential Investor

For anyone wanting to learn about the world of investing...

Table of Contents

Introduction

    Investing your money is one of the most crucial and essential things you can do when taking control of your financial future. Although for many of you starting out, this may seem complex and daunting. But with some skills and a definite plan, you can learn how to make the best choices and grow your wealth over time.

    This introduction will expose you to the basics and provide a solid foundation for anyone to start. This book will cover topics such as stocks, real estate, cryptocurrency, how to get started, and so much more! Being informed about where your money will go is essential to building wealth, whether for a retirement account or simply saving up to get a pair of shoes.

    No matter where you are in life and what you want to accomplish, these basics will help you understand how you can invest your money differently and how your risk tolerance/timing will impact how you invest your money differently.

    Thank you for taking the time to read this book, and I cannot wait for you to learn about the world of investing!

Stocks

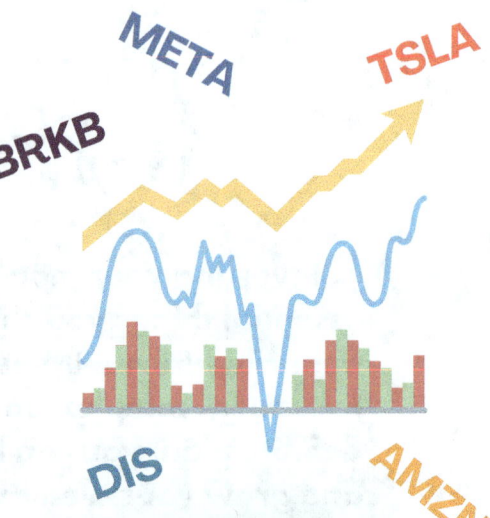

What are Stocks?

A stock represents a portion of ownership in a company and entitles the holder to the company's earnings and revenue. This is basically saying that when someone has stock, they own a part of the company and can gain or lose value depending on how the company does. Regarding generating value from stores, it's important to note that this can come from capital gains and dividends (which will be covered later in this chapter). Although stores can rise in value, knowing they can decrease is crucial. Stores can provide a more significant return than investments such as bonds, but it's important to note that they don't have equal volatility. Volatility has to deal with the stock price change (see image below). Stocks have been one of the most reliable financial vehicles and are a part of many people's investment portfolios.

In order for stock to be bought, a company has to be public. Some of the biggest public companies include: Amazon (AMZN), Meta (META), Apple(AAPL), Nike(NKE) and so many more!

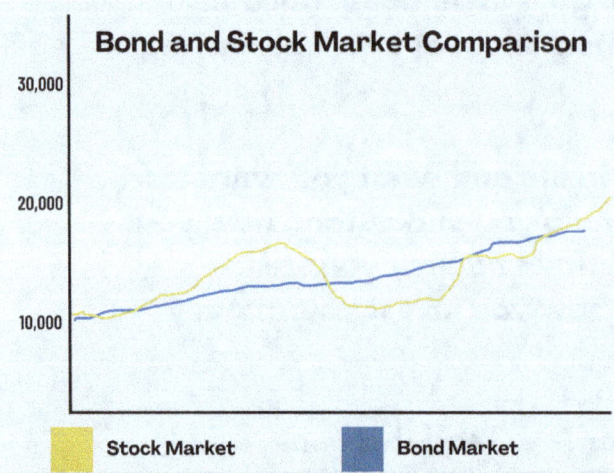

Bond and Stock Market Comparison

- Stock Market
- Bond Market

This chart shows that the blue line (Bond Market) does not have a high rate of change and overall has a linear rate of change (low volatility). On the other hand, the yellow line (Stock Market) can be seen to make more drastic changes indicating higher volatility.

Stocks are traded on the stock exchanges, such as the New York Stock Exchange (NYSE) or the NASDAQ. The value of these stocks can change due to the company's finances, economic state, and investor sentiment.

Dividends

Although money can be made from a company's capital gains, businesses will frequently offer another way for the investor to make money: through dividends. Dividends are another way shareholders get paid for owning stock and the risk within that company's stock.

Div-yield or Dividend rate is the rate the company will pay their shareholders. The div-yield of stock varies between companies. Smaller companies, with more volatility/risk, often have a higher div-yield. This is because there is a higher risk in owning the company's stock; therefore, the shareholders are rewarded more for carrying that risk. Usually, dividends are paid quarterly or every three months.

AAPL Div-yield(6/27/23)

PREVIOUS CLOSE
The last closing price: $185.27
MARKET CAP
A valuation method that multiplies the price of a company's stock by the total number of outstanding shares
2.93T USD

DIVIDEND YIELD
The ratio of the annual dividend to current share price that estimates the dividend return of a stock
0.52%
PRIMARY EXCHANGE
Listed exchange for this security
NASDAQ

This is Apple stock(AAPL) and its div-yield. The company's market cap, or as it says - A valuation method that multiplies the price of a company's stock by the total number of outstanding shares, is 2.9 Trillion US dollars. This is the most significant market cap of any stock currently in the stock market, with a div-yield of 0.52%. This is low because AAPL is less volatile and risky than other stocks.

3

Types of Stocks

People are continually trading stocks at any given moment the market is open. In the NASDAQ and NYSE, which are two of the biggest stock exchanges, there are thousands of companies that have stock. Now this may be a lot to you, but stocks can be categorized into sections:

The first type of stock is common stock. Common stock refers to the most basic form of stock. Stockholders of common stock are entitled to a portion of the company's profit and have other rights to the company, such as voting rights, ownership transfer, the right to sue, and more.

Another type of stock is preferred stock. This type of stock provides fixed dividends, paid out before ordinary stock dividends are paid. Usually, the preferred store has priority over common stock in the event of bankruptcy (when a company can no longer stay in business)or liquidation (converting assets into cash).

The third primary type of stock is growth stocks. Growth stocks are self-explanatory as they are stocks that are predicted to grow at a faster rate than the market. These stores often generate enormous profits for the holder but also have the chance to dip down a lot more. This type of stock is excellent for younger investors or investors that want to have more risk in their portfolio.

Some of the most popular stocks are called blue chip stocks. These type of stocks are from well trusted, secure and established companies. Some companies include Disney, Bank of America, Verizon, Walmart and much more.

Value stocks are stocks trading at a lower price than they should be. Investors of these stocks believe that stocks are undervalued and that their cost of them with rise, generating more significant returns.

Why do Companies go Public?

For a stock to be bought from a company, that company must go public. The public company can sell shares to investors that believe that the company will grow in value. The company can raise money for infrastructure, new products/services, and overall growth by selling shares to the public.

For example, could you take a smoothie company? The smoothie company is currently private and only has three local stores. The smoothie company is trying to expand and grow but needs more funds to grow the business. By going public, the smoothie company could raise money for new flavors, packaging, stores, employees, etc. Regarding the investor's side, the smoothie company must provide its financials so the stockholders can see how the company is doing and whether they should sell or keep the stock.

Going Public	Staying Private
• Raise Capital	• More Freedom
• More opportunities for for access to capital	• Choice on investors
• Easier for owners to sell off stock	• Less risk
• Credibility and Branding	• Easier to take over competitors
Charles Schwab	**Fidelity**

Cash and Cash Equivalents

Why is Cash and Cash Equivalents Important?

Cash Equivalents provide investors with high liquidity or how easily the asset can be converted to cash. Somewhat an amount of cash is essential in case of emergencies and simple purchases. Cash can be kept in many spots, such as bank accounts insured by the FDIC for amounts up to $250,000 or even in locked safes. Unfortunately, keeping money in banks earns little to no interest, but at least it keeps your funds safe and secure.

For very short-term investments, cash equivalents provide a safe and liquid spot to hold money. One of the most known cash equivalents is money market funds. These funds offer a slight increase in interest for your money while also allowing money to be taken out at any time.

Another cash equivalent is money market deposit accounts (MMDAs), interest-bearing deposit accounts offered by banks and financial institutions. MMDAs combine some features of both savings accounts and checking accounts, providing a balance between liquidity and earning potential. These accounts typically offer a higher interest rate than regular savings accounts while still allowing some accessibility to the funds.

US Treasury Money Market Fund

A US Treasury money market fund with checking privileges is an investment vehicle that provides investors with the benefits of both a money market fund and a checking account. These funds primarily invest in short-term US Treasury securities, considered low-risk investments.

Some examples of US Treasury securities include Treasury bills, notes, and bonds. These securities are backed by the US government, making them highly secure.

US Treasury money market funds aim to maintain a stable net asset value (NAV) of $1 per share. They focus on preserving capital and providing liquidity to investors. The underlying Treasury securities have short maturities, ensuring that funds can be readily converted to cash.

These funds also offer investors the convenience of check-writing privileges. This means that investors can write checks against their money market fund balances to make payments, transactions, or transfers, similar to a traditional checking account.

While check-writing privileges are available, there are often limitations on the number of checks written per month or the minimum check amount. These limitations aim to maintain the fund's stability and liquidity.

These funds are regulated by the Securities and Exchange Commission (SEC) and must adhere to specific guidelines to ensure the safety and transparency of the investments.

Certificates of Deposit

What are Certificates of Deposit?

Certificates of Deposit or CDs are fixed-term, interest-bearing financial instruments banks and credit unions offer. They are considered relatively low-risk investments and provide a predictable return on investment. CDs are commonly used by individuals and organizations seeking to earn interest on their savings while preserving their principal amount invested.

CDs have a specific maturity period, ranging from a few months to several years. During this time, the investor agrees not to withdraw the funds until maturity. Early withdrawals may incur penalties.

CDs offer a fixed or variable interest rate, depending on the terms and conditions set by the issuing financial institution. The interest is usually higher than regular savings accounts, with longer-term CDs generally providing higher rates. CDs offer a guaranteed return on investment. At maturity, the investor receives the initial principal amount plus accumulated interest. This predictable return makes them attractive to individuals looking for stable, low-risk investment options.

The Federal Deposit Insurance Corporation (FDIC) protects CDs offered by FDIC-insured banks. This insurance covers the maximum limit per depositor per insured bank, currently set at $250,000 per depositor.

CDs come in different types to suit different investor needs. Some common types include traditional fixed-rate CDs, variable-rate CDs, callable CDs (where the issuer can redeem the CD before maturity), and jumbo CDs (with more extensive minimum deposit requirements).

Real Estate

What is Real Estate?

Real estate investing involves acquiring, owning, and managing physical assets such as land and properties. It offers several unique characteristics that set it apart from other investment options. Investors can generate income through rental properties or profit from property value appreciation through resale. Real estate investments can range from residential properties, such as single-family homes, condos, and apartments, to commercial properties, like office buildings, retail spaces, and industrial properties. Additionally, real estate investment trusts (REITs) and real estate crowdfunding provide alternative ways to invest in the property market.

Why is Real Estate so Popular?

Real estate investing offers numerous benefits that make it an attractive investment avenue. One of the primary advantages of real estate investing is the potential for generating consistent cash flow through rental income. Owning properties and leasing them to tenants can provide a steady stream of passive income, which can be used to cover expenses, repay mortgages, and generate profits.

Real estate properties also have the potential to appreciate over time. Market conditions, location, and demand can contribute to property value appreciation, allowing investors to build equity.

Furthermore leveraging this equity through resale can result in substantial capital gains. Real estate investments offer diversification benefits with a low correlation with traditional asset classes, such as stocks and bonds. Including real estate in an investment portfolio can help mitigate risk and reduce the impact of market volatility. It is a tangible asset that can hedge against inflation and economic downturns.

Factors Influencing Real Estate Investments

The location of a property plays a crucial role in its investment potential. Analyzing economic indicators, growth prospects, job markets, and infrastructure development in a particular area can help identify lucrative investment opportunities.

Additionally, understanding supply and demand dynamics in the local market is necessary for making informed investment decisions.

Financing plays a significant role in real estate investing. Evaluating different mortgage options, interest rates, and loan terms is vital to determine the affordability and viability of an investment. Investors should consider factors such as down payment requirements, closing costs, and the impact of interest rate fluctuations on mortgage payments. Before investing in real estate, conducting proper verification is crucial. This includes property inspections, title searches, and understanding local regulations and zoning restrictions. Compliance with legal requirements and understanding potential liabilities are essential for successful real estate investing.

Risks and Challenges

Real estate markets can experience fluctuations and cyclical patterns. Economic factors, such as interest rates, employment rates, and consumer confidence, can influence property values and rental demand. Understanding these dynamics and their potential impact on investments is vital for mitigating risks. Changes in interest rates can impact mortgage affordability and the overall profitability of real estate investments. Rising interest rates can increase borrowing costs and reduce cash flow. Investors must carefully evaluate the impact of interest rate fluctuations on their investment strategy. Moreover, owning and managing properties come with responsibilities and challenges. Tenant turnover, vacancies, and maintenance expenses can impact cash flow. Property management skills, understanding tenant-landlord laws, and maintaining properties are crucial for successful real estate investing. Real estate investments are subject to legal and regulatory risks. Changes in property laws, zoning regulations, and compliance requirements can impact investments. Investors should stay informed about legal obligations and seek professional advice to alleviate potential risks.

Types of Real Estate

There are many real estate types, but the three main types are residential, commercial, and industrial. Many people see real estate as a valuable investment since it can generate income through rent or appreciation in value over time.

Residential

Residential real estate is the properties used for living purposes, such as apartments, houses, townhouses, condos, etc. Some specific examples include:

- Single-family home: A home occupied by one family.
- Multi-family home: A building with separate living units made for multiple families.
- Duplexes: A building that contains two separate living units, each with its entrance.
- Condominiums: A multi-unit building where each unit is connected to hallways and amenities with other owners.

Commercial

Commercial real estate is buildings used for business purposes, such as retail stores, office buildings, and other commercial properties. Some specific examples include:

- Office buildings: A multi-story building used for office space, such as corporate offices, law firms, etc.
- Retail spaces are used for retail businesses such as stores, shops, and malls.
- Hotels: A building providing a temporary place for travelers to lodge.
- Restaurants: A property used for serving food and beverages to customers.

Industrial

Industrial real estate refers to the buildings used for manufacturing and storing, such as factories, warehouses, and distribution centers. Some examples include:

- Factories: A large building used for creating and producing goods
- Warehouses: A facility used to store goods
- Distribution centers: A commercial building that sends goods and supplies, usually for a larger supply chain.
- Industrial properties: buildings that both store and produce goods.

REITs

Real Estate Investment Trusts or REITs own, operate, or finance income-producing properties such as apartments, hotels, office buildings, shopping centers, and warehouses. REITs allow investors to invest in real estate properties and earn income from rental income, interest income, or capital appreciation.

Housing Market

Real estate has been one of the best investments for years through inflation and deflation. No matter what the housing price has gone up, real estate has always been a good investment for investors. A big part of real estate is that people always need a home, so someone will always be in the market for a house, whether a couple or a family.

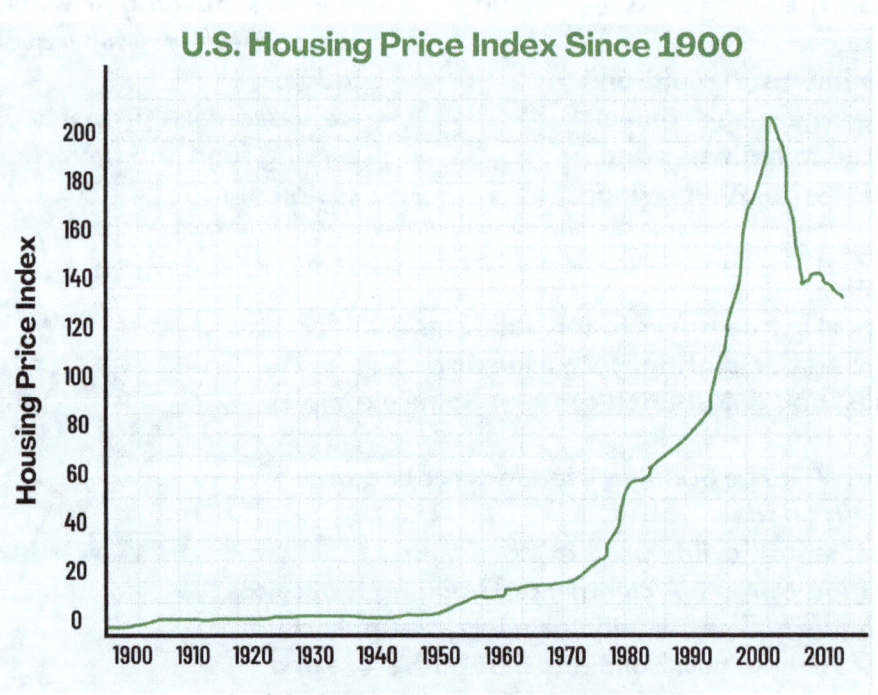

A graph of the housing market from 1900-2010.

Bonds

What is a Bond?

During WW1, liberty bonds were given to the citizens of America to fund the war. After a couple of years, the citizens would get paid back some money with interest, ultimately leading to a profit. When the government or a corporation wants to raise money, they will issue bonds, saying that in a few years, you can cash in the money on a maturity date. Bonds are often seen as some of the most reliable and stable investments as they usually maintain a constant growth rate and don't have much volatility.

Types of Bonds

Government	Coporate	Municipal
Government bonds are bonds issued by the government and are said to be low risk. They are low risk due to the fact that they can tax citizens to make up for the debt. Normally government bonds have a fixed rate of interest, meaning the interest paid will not change.	Corporate bonds are issued by companies to raise capital. Often times these may be riskier, but they yield higher profits. These types of bonds can mature short-term and even long term (30+ years).	Municipal bonds are issued by state and local government, and raise money for public projects such as programs, repairs, bridges schools, streets etc. Municipal bonds are re- exempt from federal income tax making a good investment for "tax-conscious" investors.

Why Bonds?

Bonds mathematically work meaning that they can do well when taking into consideration their risk levels. Bonds are often an excellent investment for people who don't want to take much risk and still want to invest such as the elderly.

13

Risks of investing in bonds

1. Interest rate risk
2. Call risk
3. Volatility risk
4. Inflation risk
5. Default risk

1. <u>Interest-rate risk</u>

As interest rates rise, the value of a bond will fall. If an investor has to sell a bond before the maturity date, the investor will see a capital loss. (The significant risk faced by investors in the bond market.)

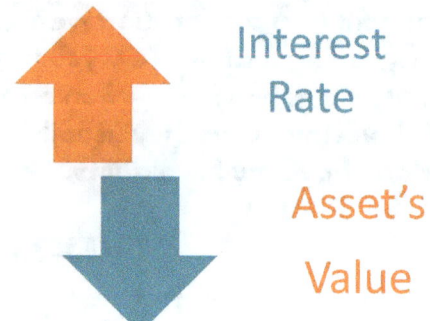

Interest Rate

Asset's Value

2. <u>Call Risk</u>

Many bonds include a provision that allows the issuer to retire/call all or part of the issue before the maturity date. The issuer usually has this right to have the flexibility to refinance the bond in the future if the market interest rate drops below the coupon rate.

3. <u>Volatility Risk</u>

The risk is that a change in volatility will affect the price of a bond adversely. One of the factors is the volatility of interest rates.

4. Inflation Risk

The risk is that inflation exceeds the coupon rate. Inflationary risk refers to the risk that inflation will undermine the performance of an investment, the value of an asset, or the purchasing power of a stream of income. Looking at financial results without taking into account inflation is the nominal return. The value an investor should worry about is the purchasing power, referred to as the actual return.

5. Default Risk

The risk is that the bond issuer may default(they will not be able to make the principal and interest payments.) Bonds with default risk trade at a lower rate compared to US treasury securities. Us treasury securities are "risk-free". Junk Bonds: High-yield, risky for the issuer to pay back.

Index and Mutual Funds

What are Index and Mutual Funds?

Index and Mutual Funds are investment funds that pool money from multiple investors to purchase a diverse portfolio of securities.

- Track performance of specific markets such as the S&P 500

- Passively Managed

- Lower Fees (Less managed)

- Index Funds returns are based of the index or market they are in

- Dow Jones Industrial Average

- Provide a wide range of securities
- Pool money from investors
- Provide high diversification
- High Liquidity(Can be bought and sold almost any time)

- Can use different financial strategy and not track a market

- Actively Managed

- Higher Fees (Managed)

- Mutual funds are riskier but also can provided higher yields

Index Funds   **Mutual Funds**

Instead of the stress of deciding what particular stock to choose, index funds provide a variety of the top companies for investors to have a share in. These types of investments are often consistent and deliver positive results as companies are usually growing and gaining capital.

ETFs

What is an ETF?

An ETF, or an exchange-traded fund, works much like a mutual fund, except you can buy or sell it throughout the day, just like any stock. An ETF can be structured to track anything from the price of an individual stock or commodity to a large and diverse collection of securities. Also, ETFs can be structured to follow individual stocks, commodities, and more. The first ever ETF was the SPY(SPDR) ETF, which tracks and follows the S&P 500.

An ETF is a basket of securities traded daily like any standard stock while share prices fluctuates throughout the day. ETFs don't have only to be stocks; they can also be bonds and many other types of investments. These offer lower expense ratios, and you don't have to pay all the commissions you typically would with a broker(many brokers no longer have commissions).

There are many ETFs; Passive and Active, Bonds, Stocks, Industry sector, Commodity, Currency, Inverse, and Leveraged ETFs.

There must be diversification within funds to maintain a healthy portfolio. Equity, bond, hybrid, and money market funds are the main and, ideally the best ones to look at. Funds are typically made up of different stocks and securities, so they are typically lower risk than individual stocks and are more diverse. However, it is still essential to have different kinds of bonds for safety reasons.

Cryptocurrency

What is Cryptocurrency

Cryptocurrencies are digital assets based on cryptography and decentralized blockchain technology. They enable secure, transparent, and peer-to-peer transactions without intermediaries. Bitcoin (BTC) is the pioneering cryptocurrency, but numerous alternative cryptocurrencies (altcoins) and stablecoins serve various purposes in the digital asset ecosystem. Additionally, cryptocurrencies have facilitated tokenization and the development of decentralized applications (DApps) through smart contracts.

A blockchain is a massive part of cryptocurrency transactions. A blockchain is a digital log of transactions made in a network. Once a transaction is made, it is broadcasted to the web and verified. These transactions are all visible to the participants of the network. Within a blockchain, you know that you are secure and transparent. Trust and transparency are built within the community since there is not just one person in control.

With the rise in popularity of Cryptocurrency recently, it's essential to avoid falling for scams or Ponzi schemes. With the amount of money people made during the crypto bull market, people are willing to take advantage of this and use other people's money to benefit themselves and not others.

18

Why Cryptocurrency?

Cryptocurrencies have witnessed significant price appreciation over the years, providing investors with the potential for substantial returns. Early adoption and market growth have contributed to these opportunities. Cryptocurrency markets are accessible globally and operate 24/7, allowing investors to trade anytime. Additionally, cryptocurrencies provide high liquidity, enabling investors to buy or sell assets quickly and efficiently. Cryptocurrencies correlate poorly with traditional asset classes such as stocks and bonds, making them valuable to diversified investment portfolios. They can act as a hedge against inflation and economic instability.

The first transaction involving Bitcoin was made on May 22, 2010, when Laszlo Hanyecz, a programmer, purchased two pizzas for 10,000 Bitcoins. This transaction is widely regarded as the first real-world transaction using Bitcoin as a medium of exchange. At the time, the value of 10,000 Bitcoins was relatively insignificant, but in today's market, it would be worth millions of dollars. This event is often celebrated as "Bitcoin Pizza Day" within the cryptocurrency community.

Risks and Challenges

Cryptocurrency markets are known for their price volatility and cycles of boom and bust. The high-risk, high-reward nature of cryptocurrencies necessitates a careful approach. Regulatory frameworks for cryptocurrencies vary globally, leading to uncertainty and potential compliance risks. The evolving nature of regulations can impact the market and investors' ability to participate. Cryptocurrencies face technological challenges such as scalability and transaction speed. Network vulnerabilities and software bugs can also affect the stability and functionality of cryptocurrencies.

In 2017, a British man named James Howells accidentally threw away a hard drive containing 7,500 bitcoins. At the time, the bitcoins were worth around $4 million. Howells realized his mistake when he saw the rising value of Bitcoin in the news. He desperately tried to locate the hard drive, but unfortunately, it ended up in a landfill. Despite offering to donate a portion of the recovered bitcoins to the local council, his request to search the landfill was denied due to environmental and safety concerns. This incident is a cautionary tale highlighting the importance of securely storing and backing up cryptocurrency assets.

What is an NFT?

An NFT, or non-fungible token, is a digital asset representing ownership or proof of authenticity of a unique item or piece of content. Unlike cryptocurrencies such as Bitcoin or Ethereum, which are fungible and can be exchanged like-for-like, NFTs are indivisible and cannot be mutually exchanged. Each NFT has a distinct value and specific characteristics that make it different from other tokens.

Here are a few ways people can make money with NFTs:

- **Creating and Selling NFTs:** Artists and content creators can mint their work as NFTs and sell them on various NFT marketplaces. When someone purchases their NFT, the creator receives a percentage of the sale price as a royalty fee.

- **Trading NFTs:** Similar to traditional asset trading, people can buy NFTs at a lower price and sell them at a higher price, aiming to profit from the price appreciation. NFTs can be traded on dedicated marketplaces or through peer-to-peer transactions.

- **Royalties and Resales:** Creators can include royalty fees in the intelligent contracts of their NFTs. This allows them to earn a percentage of subsequent sales whenever their NFT is resold on the secondary market.

- **Gaming and Virtual Worlds:** NFTs are increasingly utilized in video games and virtual worlds, where players can buy, sell, and trade in-game assets or virtual land. Some games allow players to earn real money by selling their acquired NFTs.

- **Tokenized Collectibles:** Collectibles, such as sports memorabilia or rare digital items, can be tokenized as NFTs. These unique collectibles can appreciate over time, and owners can profit by selling them to interested buyers.

What is DeFi?

DeFi, or decentralized finance, is built with blockchain technology. In a DeFi system, financial applications and services are built on top of decentralized blockchain platforms, allowing users to interact directly with each other without the need for a central authority or intermediary. This is achieved through smart contracts, and self-executing programs that automatically execute financial transactions based on pre-defined rules.

- - - - - - - - - - - - - - - - - -

Cryptocurrencies have disrupted the traditional investment landscape, offering potentially high returns, accessibility, and portfolio diversification. Understanding the fundamental concepts, risks, and investment strategies associated with cryptocurrencies is crucial for navigating this volatile market. As with any investment, conducting thorough research, practicing risk management, and staying informed about market developments is essential. By embracing the potential of cryptocurrencies while acknowledging the associated risks, investors can explore this evolving asset class and potentially unlock new opportunities for wealth generation.

Retirement Accounts

What are Retirement Accounts?

A type of investment account known as a retirement account is created specifically to assist people in saving for their retirement. The purpose of retirement accounts is to help people save for their future needs by offering tax advantages and other benefits.

Many types of retirement accounts exist, and employers or financial institutions frequently provide them. Retirement accounts can be divided into several categories, including 401(k)s, IRAs (Individual Retirement Accounts), Roth IRAs, and Solo 401(k)s.

401(k)

A 401(k) is a retirement account that lets employees contribute to a beneficial advantage investment account. With this, many employees can save money over time once they retire. Often, these contributions are taken directly out of the employee's payroll, and many employers match contributions up to a certain percentage. For a 401(k), there is a limit to how much you can put in each year. As of 2023, an investor can put in$22,500, and people above 50 can put in an extra $7,500 yearly.

Solo 401(k)

A Solo 401(k) is a retirement account for small business owners and self-employed individuals. Similar to the standard 401(k) retirement account, contributions can be made with pre-tax dollars while the money grows tax-deferred. In a Solo 401(k), a high contribution limit allows for greater returns for the individual.

Traditional IRA

A Traditional IRA is a personal retirement account that is tax-advantageous. The money in the account also grows tax-deferred, meaning you don't pay any taxes on the earnings until you cash out. Usually, for Traditional IRAs, more investment choices provide options and flexibility. As of 2023, an investor can put in$6,500, and people above 50 can $7,500 each year.

Roth IRA

A Roth IRA is a retirement account where contributions are made with after-tax dollars. But on the other hand, the money grows tax-free, so you will never have to pay any tax after you withdraw, meaning whatever is in that account is yours to keep.

What is a 401k?

Benefits

1. Tax advantages: Contributions to a 401(k) are made on a pre-tax basis, meaning they are deducted from your income before taxes are calculated. This can reduce your taxable income in the current year, potentially lowering your tax bill. Additionally, the money in your 401(k) account grows tax-free until you withdraw it in retirement.
2. Employer matching: Many employers offer to match a portion of their employees' 401(k) contributions, which can be a significant source of additional savings.

3. Automatic savings: With a 401(k) plan, your contributions are automatically deducted from your paycheck, making it easier to save for the future.
4. Investment options: Most 401(k) plans offer various investment options, such as mutual funds and index funds, which can help you build a diversified portfolio.

How to Start/Requirements

Check Eligibility: Confirm if your employer offers a 401k plan and determine if you meet the eligibility requirements. Some employers may require you to have worked for a certain period or reach a minimum age before you can participate.

1. Check Eligibility
2. Review Plan details
3. Enroll in the plan
4. Determine Contribution amount
5. Employee Matching
6. Choose Investment options
7. Manage account

What is a Roth IRA?

Requirements/Restrictions

Minimum Income
The amount you put in your brokerage account in one year must be less than your earned income in that given year. For most people, this seems very easy and almost impossible for people to even do, but for children that have saved money over time and want to place it into a Roth IRA, it must be less than their income.

Maximum Income
There is a maximum amount of money you can make from your outside job in which you will not be allowed to put money into your Roth IRA. If you make over $144,000 in a year in 2022, you can not put any money into your Roth IRA. *For 2023, it will be changed to $153,000 per year. This does not mean your account will cease to exist, but it means you can no longer contribute money. That's why starting as young as possible is the best thing you can do.

Maximum Contributions
The maximum amount you can put into your account is $6,000 if you are under 50. If you are above age 50, you can put up to $7,000. *This is as of 2022. In 2023, it will be $6,500 for people under 50 and $7,500 for people over 50. This changes year to year and will likely become more extensive due to inflation and interest rates.

As the cost of living continues to increase, relying on just social security or a pension plan will be challenging. Also, living on the bare minimum could be possible for those who rely so heavily on social security or a pension plan. Contributing a small amount every month at a young age will build up in the account and allow a tax-free retirement withdrawal (age 60 for most Roth IRAs).

How to get started with a Roth IRA

1. <u>Determine your eligibility:</u> To open a Roth IRA, you must meet specific criteria. You must have earned income (such as wages, salary, or self-employment income), and your income must fall within the limits set by the IRS. The limits change each year, so check the current limits.
2. <u>Choose a financial institution:</u> Look for a reputable institution offering Roth IRAs. Options include banks, credit unions, brokerage firms, and online investment platforms. Compare their fees, investment options, customer service, and any additional features they may offer.
3. <u>Gather necessary information:</u> You'll need to provide personal information, including your Social Security number, date of birth, and contact information. Be prepared to provide identification documents to comply with anti-money laundering regulations.

4. <u>Complete the application:</u> Fill out the application form provided by your chosen financial institution. Depending on the institution, this may be done online or through paper forms. Read the terms and conditions carefully before submitting your application

5. <u>Fund your Roth IRA:</u> Decide how much money you want to contribute to your Roth IRA. The IRS sets maximum contribution limits each year, so make sure you are within those limits. You can contribute cash or transfer funds from another retirement account (e.g., a traditional IRA or a 401(k)) into your Roth IRA.

6. <u>Select your investments:</u> Once your Roth IRA is funded, you must choose how to invest the money within the account. Most financial institutions offer a range of investment options, such as stocks, bonds, mutual funds, or exchange-traded funds (ETFs). Please take a look at your risk tolerance, time horizon, and investment goals when making your selections.

Pensions

What are Pensions?

Pensions are retirement benefit plans that provide individuals with a regular income during their retirement years. They are designed to help individuals maintain their standard of living and meet their financial needs after they stop working. Employers, government entities, or other organizations typically offer pensions as part of an employee's compensation package.

Many pensions are employer-sponsored retirement plans. Employers contribute a portion of the employee's compensation into a pension fund throughout their working years. These contributions are often based on salary, years of service, and the specific pension plan's rules.

There are two primary types of pension plans: defined benefit and defined contribution.

    a. Defined Benefit: The employer guarantees a specific retirement benefit based on a predetermined formula in a defined benefit plan. This formula typically considers factors such as salary history, years of service, and a specific percentage multiplier. The employer bears the investment and longevity risk, and retirees receive a fixed amount for the rest of their lives.

    b. Defined Contribution: In a defined contribution plan, the employer, employee, or both contribute funds into an individual retirement account. The final pension benefit depends on the contributions made and the account's investment performance. The employee assumes the investment risk, and the eventual retirement income will vary based on the account's value at retirement.

Pensions often have a vesting period, the duration of service required for an employee to become eligible for the employer's contributions. Once an employee becomes vested, they are entitled to the benefits accrued in the pension plan.

Pension contributions made by employers or employees may be tax-deductible, reducing taxable income in the current year. However, pension income received during retirement is typically subject to income tax.

Pensions also provide regular income to retirees. The frequency and duration of payments can vary, but they are typically monthly and continue for the retiree's lifetime. Some pension plans also offer joint and survivor benefits options, allowing a portion of the pension income to continue for a spouse or beneficiary after the retiree's death.

Depending on the pension plan, individuals may have options to take their pension benefits with them if they change jobs. This may involve rolling over the pension funds into an individual retirement account (IRA) or another qualified retirement plan.

In some cases, pensions may be integrated with Social Security benefits. This means the pension amount may be adjusted based on the retiree's Social Security income.

Pensions play a vital role in retirement planning, providing individuals with a stable source of income to support their financial needs in their post-employment years. However, the availability and structure of pensions can vary across different countries, employers, and industries. Individuals must understand their specific pension plan terms, eligibility criteria, contribution requirements, and projected retirement income.

Investment Options within Retirement Accounts

Retirement accounts provide opportunities to diversify investments across various asset classes, such as stocks, bonds, mutual funds, and exchange-traded funds (ETFs). Proper asset allocation can help manage risk and optimize returns based on individual risk tolerance and time horizon. Mutual funds and ETFs offer access to professionally managed portfolios. These investment vehicles pool funds from multiple investors, providing diversification and the expertise of professional fund managers. For individuals comfortable with self-directed investing, retirement accounts can also accommodate investments in individual stocks and bonds. This option requires research, knowledge, and careful consideration of risk.

Target-date funds are investment options that automatically adjust asset allocation based on an individual's projected retirement date. These funds become more conservative as the target date approaches, minimizing risk exposure.

Strategies for Optimizing Retirement Savings

Contributing the maximum allowable amount to retirement accounts each year is crucial for building substantial savings. This includes taking advantage of employer matching contributions, which can significantly boost retirement savings. Periodic portfolio review and rebalancing ensure that the asset allocation remains aligned with long-term goals and risk tolerance. Rebalancing helps maintain the desired investment mix and manage risk exposure. Understanding the rules and deadlines for required minimum distributions (RMDs) is crucial. RMDs are the minimum amount individuals must withdraw from their retirement accounts once they reach a certain age.

F.I.R.E. Movement

What is F.I.R.E?

The FIRE (Financial Independence, Retire Early) movement is a lifestyle and financial strategy to achieve financial independence and retire early. It emphasizes aggressive saving, frugal living, and strategic investing to accumulate enough wealth to support a comfortable lifestyle without needing traditional employment.
Here's a breakdown of the fundamental principles and strategies often associated with the FIRE movement:

- **Financial Independence:** FIRE proponents strive to reach a point where they have accumulated enough wealth and passive income streams to cover their living expenses without relying on a traditional job. This financial independence provides the flexibility to pursue other interests and activities.

- **Aggressive Saving:** FIRE advocates the importance of saving a significant portion of income, often targeting a savings rate of 50% or more. Individuals can accelerate their path to financial independence by minimizing expenses and maximizing savings.

- **Frugal Living:** Living below one's means is fundamental to the FIRE movement. FIRE followers typically adopt a minimalist lifestyle, cutting back on unnecessary expenses and prioritizing saving and investing over material possessions.

- Investment Strategy: Investing is a crucial component of the FIRE movement. Followers aim to grow their wealth by investing in a diversified portfolio of assets, such as stocks, bonds, real estate, and index funds. The goal is to generate passive income and increase net worth over time.

- Retiring Early: The FIRE movement's ultimate objective is to bed early, typically in their 40s or 50s. Individuals can pursue other interests, work part-time, or retire by achieving financial independence and accumulating sufficient wealth.

It's important to note that the FIRE movement requires discipline, careful planning, and a long-term perspective. It may not be suitable for everyone, as it often involves making significant lifestyle changes and sacrificing immediate gratification for long-term financial freedom. Additionally, the movement's principles can vary among individuals, and there is no one-size-fits-all approach.

If you're considering pursuing FIRE, conducting thorough research, seeking professional financial advice, and developing a comprehensive financial plan that aligns with your goals, risk tolerance, and individual circumstances is advisable.

Investment Strategy

The way you invest can be very different compared to other individuals. How you invest can change depending on your financial capital, age, income, risk tolerance, personality, and more. For example, older people won't take as much risk in their investments, while young people will often be riskier as they have time to make up for losses when they get older. Depending on one's circumstances and goals, investing can be very different.

Fundamental Investment Strategies

An investing strategy called Value investing involves identifying undervalued assets with growth potential. Investors employing this strategy analyze financial metrics and company fundamentals to identify stocks or assets trading below their intrinsic value. Value investors seek to capitalize on future price appreciation by investing in undervalued assets.

Growth investing focuses on companies with high growth potential. Investors employing this strategy look for companies expected to experience above-average growth rates compared to the overall market. Evaluating future earnings prospects and industry trends is vital in identifying promising growth stocks.

Income investing aims to generate regular income streams from investments. This strategy often involves investing in dividend-paying stocks, bonds, or real estate investment trusts (REITs). Income investors seek assets that provide consistent income while maintaining a reasonable level of risk. Index investing involves investing in broad market indexes to achieve market returns. Instead of selecting individual stocks, investors opt for index funds or exchange-traded funds (ETFs) that track the performance of specific market indexes. This strategy provides diversification and helps investors capture the overall market returns.

Asset Allocation

Asset Allocation refers to how you diversify your assets within your investment portfolio. By diversifying your investment portfolio into assets such as stocks, bonds, real estate, etc, you can have multiple sources of income and protection from loss of income. By diversifying, you balance your risk into categories instead of just one. For example, if an individual puts all their money into real estate, and then the housing market crashes, a significant loss will occur that will be difficult to come back from when all you had to do is allocate your assets and manage your risks.

Dollar Cost Averaging

One of the most popular and effective ways of investing is by dollar cost averaging. Dollar-cost averaging is when you have a fixed amount of money you will invest on a set schedule in a particular security, no matter the price. For example, say that you were given $800. You could invest it all at once at the current share price and hope it goes up. But what if the price went down or stayed the same, and you lost lots of money or made no gain? Here is where dollar cost averaging comes in. Instead of one contribution of $800, you could invest $100 every month. This would be beneficial because when the share price goes down the next month, you can buy it for cheaper and gain the profits from that purchase.

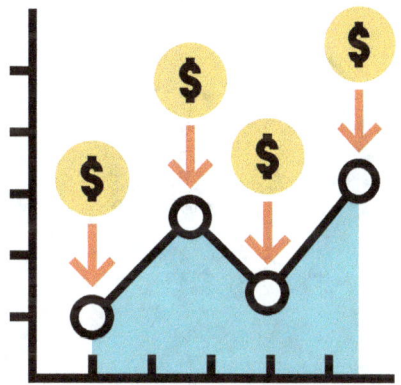

Day Trading

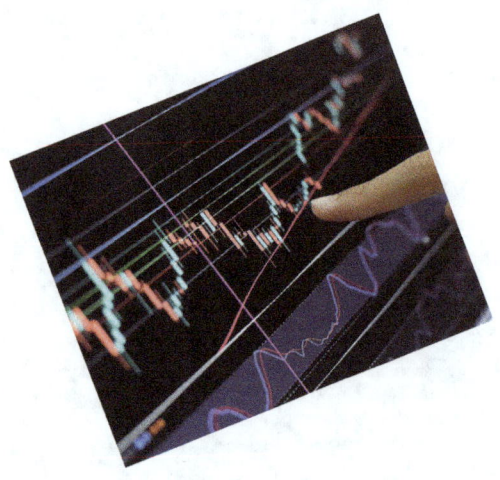

Day trading is the idea of buying and selling stocks, currencies, commodities, etc., within a day. Day trading is known to be much riskier than buying and holding but has been seen to produce high returns. The investments day traders make are often short-term, as day traders always buy and sell assets. Day trading can get complicated through technical analysis where you use strategies to predict how the market will change and measure volatility. It's important to note that when day trading, some constant commissions, and fees must be paid frequently, which can slowly eat into the profits made by the investor.

Buy and Hold investing is one of the safest ways to invest as you buy an asset and never sell it, regardless of short-term market fluctuations. In the long term, you will earn money because you are never really buying and selling stocks.

Another strategy of investing is buying on margin. One of the riskier ways of investing, but buying on margin is taking out a loan and essentially not investing your own money. This money is usually lent by a broker who will charge interest on the loan. This can be risky because if you lose the money you will owe a lot more than if you just used your own.

International Investing

International Investing

International Investing is investing in assets such as stocks, bonds, commodities, or other securities issued by companies or governments in other places other than one's home country. International investing can provide things such as diversification and greater returns. Emerging economies such as China, Brazil, the Philippines, etc, provided investors with opportunities to invest in and allow individuals to diversify their assets among different nations. On the other hand, international investing can have challenges and risks, such as cultural barriers, political issues, conflicts, currency risk, and sometimes even higher costs/fees.

There are many ways for people to invest internationally, such as through real estate, ETFs, ADRs, bonds, and even through an IRA. When it comes to international investing, it's crucial that you do your research, as countries have many different economies that can impact you financially. And even international markets can impact personal home country markets. Take the war between Russia and Ukraine. The war happened in Europe, but the actions and events during the war impacted countries like the U.S. and their oil prices increased because Russia was no longer supplying the U.S., impacting the American economy.

Long Term vs Short Term Investing

Long Term vs Short Term

As previously said, investing is based on your goals and risk tolerance. Long-term and short-term investing are two different approaches to investing, each with advantages and disadvantages.

Long Term Investing

Long-term investing is holding onto an investment for more than a year. Long-term investing primarily focuses on generating wealth over time through compounding returns. Some examples of long-term investments include stocks, bonds, mutual funds, exchange-traded funds (ETFs), real estate, and retirement accounts.

Pros	Cons
• Typically less volatile and less affected by short-term changes in the market • Brokerage fees and transactions costs are lower • It doesn't have to be constantly managed • Potential for steady and higher returns	• Requires patience as returns can take longer to be generated • Lower Liquidity • Can have high risk due to economies and geopolitical events.

36

Short Term Investing

Short-term investing refers to buying and selling investments within a short time, usually less than a year. The primary target for short-term investing is to make quick returns from market fluctuations. This involves timing the market and entering and leaving the market frequently. Some examples of short-term investing are day trading, options trading, certificates of deposit (CDs), high-yield savings accounts, and flipping real estate.

Pros	Cons
• Potential for quick and easy profits as returns are made much quicker • Higher Liquidity as investments can be converted to cash more easier • Flexibility and ability to make rapid changes	• Higher risk due to volatility and risk • High fees and transaction costs because of the volume of purchases made • Time-consuming • It has to be frequently managed and kept organized • Emotions can play a role in what you invest in

Master Limited Partnerships

What are Master Limited Partnerships?

Master Limited Partnerships (MLPs) are publicly traded partnerships operating in the energy infrastructure sector. MLPs are primarily involved in transporting, storing, and processing natural resources, such as oil, gas, and other energy commodities. They allow investors to participate in the energy industry while enjoying certain tax advantages and potential income through regular distributions.

MLPs are structured as limited partnerships, consisting of two types of partners: general and limited. The general partner manages the day-to-day operations of the MLP and is responsible for decision-making, while limited partners provide capital and have limited liability.

One significant advantage of MLPs is their tax structure. MLPs are exempt from paying corporate income taxes at the entity level. Instead, the tax liability passes through to individual investors responsible for paying taxes on their share of the MLP's income. This structure can potentially result in tax advantages for investors, as they may be able to offset their taxable income with available deductions.

Like any investment, MLPs carry certain risks that investors should consider. These may include commodity price volatility, regulatory changes, interest rate fluctuations, and operational risks associated with the energy industry. Additionally, MLP distributions can be impacted by changes in the MLP's financial performance or its ability to generate sufficient cash flows.

38

Commodities

What are commodities?

Commodities are raw materials or agricultural products that can be bought and sold on markets. Commodities are traded worldwide and can be affected by many factors, such as weather, government policies, and trends.

Commodities are a great way of diversifying one's portfolio as they can fight against inflation. Although this is often true, commodities' prices can be unpredictable and volatile.

There are many commodities, such as energy, precious metals, industrial metals, agriculture, livestock, and soft commodities.

Energy	Precious Metals	Industrial Metals
• Crude Oil	• Gold	• Copper
• Heating Oil	• Silver	• Aluminum
• Gasoline	• Platinum	• Nickel
• Electricity	• Palladium	• Zinc
	• Rhodium	• Lead

Agriculture	Livestock	Soft Commodities
• Corn	• Cattle	• Coffee
• Wheat	• Sheep	• Sugar
• Rice	• Goats	• Cotton
• Hay	• Poultry	• Rice
• Soybeans		• Wheat

39

Energy (Commodities)

Energy commodities refer to raw materials used to produce and deliver energy, serving as the backbone of various industries. The primary types of energy commodities include crude oil, natural gas, coal, and electricity. The significance of renewable energy commodities such as solar, wind, and biofuels is explored.

Understanding the supply and demand dynamics of energy commodities is crucial for investors. Factors that drive energy prices include geopolitical events, production levels, economic indicators, technological advancements, environmental policies, and weather patterns. The intricate relationship between these factors shapes the volatility and profitability of energy investments.

Traditional Energy Commodities

Crude oil is the most widely traded and influential energy commodity. The extraction, refining, pricing mechanisms, and global supply chains associated with crude oil are explored. OPEC decisions, geopolitical tensions, and demand fluctuations significantly impact crude oil prices. The impact of sustainability concerns and the transition towards cleaner alternatives on the crude oil market is also examined. Natural gas is a versatile and increasingly important energy source. The exploration, production, transportation, and pricing dynamics of natural gas are delved into. The growing demand for natural gas as a cleaner alternative to coal and advancements in liquefied natural gas (LNG) technology has transformed the natural gas market. Factors such as seasonal demand, infrastructure developments, and regulatory policies affecting natural gas prices are analyzed. Coal remains a significant energy commodity, particularly in developing economies. The extraction methods, global reserves, and the environmental implications associated with its use are explored. The evolving role of coal in the energy mix, along with factors such as government regulations and shifts towards cleaner alternatives, is essential for assessing coal investments.

Renewable Energy Commodities

Solar energy has emerged as a prominent renewable energy source. The technology advancements, cost trends, and policy support driving the solar energy market are examined. Government incentives, technological innovations, and integrating solar energy into the grid impact solar investments' profitability and growth potential.

Wind energy has experienced rapid growth, becoming a key player in the renewable energy landscape. The development of wind power, including onshore and offshore wind farms, turbine technology, and regional variations, is explored. Factors such as wind resource availability, government policies, and grid infrastructure influence the economics of wind energy investments.

Biofuels offer an alternative to fossil fuels by utilizing organic matter as an energy source. The production processes, feedstock types, and regulatory frameworks that shape the biofuels market are delved into. Factors such as government mandates, feedstock availability, and advancements in biofuel technologies affect the viability of biofuel investments.

- -

Energy commodities present a dynamic and multifaceted investment landscape. Understanding the drivers, risks, and opportunities associated with traditional and renewable energy commodities is essential for investors seeking exposure to the energy sector. By carefully analyzing market dynamics, regulatory factors, and emerging trends, investors can make informed decisions that align with their financial objectives and contribute to the global transition towards sustainable and clean energy sources.

Precious Metals (Commodities)

Precious metals are rare and naturally occurring elements with high economic value. The four primary precious metals: gold, silver, platinum, and palladium. Each metal possesses distinct properties, historical significance, and industrial applications, contributing to its market demand and investment appeal.

Gold

Gold has been revered throughout history for its beauty and enduring value. Gold has historical uses including currency standards, jewelry, and store of value. Its unique properties, scarcity, and cultural significance contribute to its enduring investment appeal. Various factors, including economic indicators, inflation expectations, interest rates, currency movements, and geopolitical risks influence gold prices.

Silver

Silver is a versatile precious metal with applications in various industries, including electronics, solar panels, and medical devices. Silver's dual nature as an industrial and investment metal is also critical. Factors such as technological advancements, economic growth, and supply-demand dynamics shape the investment opportunities in silver.

Platinum and Palladium

Platinum and palladium are primarily used in the automotive industry, particularly catalytic converters. These metals are crucial in reducing harmful emissions and gaining significance in transitioning toward cleaner technologies. As such, they offer unique investment potential. Factors such as global vehicle production, emission regulations, mining supply, and overall economic conditions influence platinum and palladium prices. Understanding these market influences is crucial for identifying investment opportunities and managing risks.

Risks and Considerations

Investing in precious metals is not without risks. Price volatility is inherent in these markets, and factors such as economic downturns, changes in investor sentiment, or unexpected geopolitical events can impact prices. Understanding these risks is essential for making informed investment decisions. Physical ownership of precious metals requires careful consideration of storage and custodial options. Investors need to assess secure storage solutions, such as vaults, safe deposit boxes, or custodial services, and consider insurance coverage to safeguard their holdings.

Industrial Metals (Commodities)

Industrial metals are non-precious metals that find extensive use in manufacturing, construction, and infrastructure projects. Copper, aluminum, zinc, nickel, and lead are the primary industrial metals with distinct properties and industrial applications. The demand for industrial metals is closely linked to global economic activity, particularly in the construction, automotive, electronics, and energy sectors. Market dynamics are influenced by factors such as GDP growth, infrastructure development, technological advancements, and government policies.

Copper

Copper is widely used in electrical wiring, plumbing, infrastructure, and electronics. The metal's excellent conductivity and corrosion resistance make it indispensable in numerous industries. Investors can gain exposure to copper through various avenues, including future contracts, exchange-traded products, and mining company stocks. Factors such as supply-demand dynamics, global economic trends, and infrastructure development projects must be evaluated when considering copper as an investment.

Aluminum

Aluminum's lightweight and corrosion-resistant properties make it popular in transportation, aerospace, packaging, and construction. The metal's versatility, recyclability, and cost-effectiveness contribute to its widespread use. Investors can gain exposure to aluminum through futures contracts, ETFs, or investing in aluminum-producing companies. Considerations include global aluminum supply and demand dynamics, energy costs, technological advancements, and aluminum recycling trends.

Zinc, Nickel, and Lead

Zinc, nickel, and lead have various industrial applications. Zinc is primarily used for galvanizing steel, nickel is used in stainless steel and batteries, and information is used in batteries, construction, and ammunition. The prices of zinc, nickel, and lead are influenced by factors such as industrial production, infrastructure projects, energy costs, and geopolitical events. Monitoring these market drivers helps investors make informed decisions.

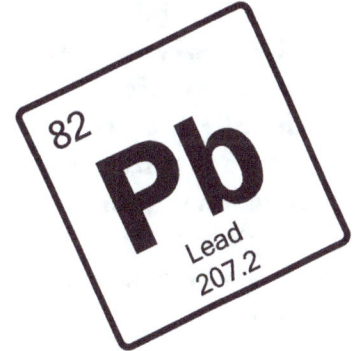

Agriculture/Livestock/Soft Commodities (Commodities)

Agricultural commodities encompass a broad range of products derived from farming, including grains (such as corn, wheat, and rice), oilseeds (like soybeans and canola), livestock (including cattle, hogs, and poultry), and soft commodities (such as coffee, cocoa, sugar, and cotton). Each category holds its own unique characteristics and investment potential. The agricultural market is subject to various dynamics and factors that influence prices. These include weather conditions, global supply and demand, crop diseases, government policies, trade regulations, and changing consumer preferences.

Grains and Oilseeds

Grains and oilseeds are fundamental staples in the global food supply chain. They serve as essential ingredients in various food products and feed for livestock. Population growth, dietary changes, and economic development influence the demand for these commodities. Investors can gain exposure to grains and oilseeds through futures contracts, exchange-traded funds (ETFs), or agricultural commodity-focused mutual funds. Factors to consider include crop production outlook, weather patterns, global trade dynamics, and government policies affecting agriculture.

46

Livestock

Livestock commodities, including cattle, hogs, and poultry, are significant in meeting global protein consumption. Rising incomes, urbanization, and changing dietary preferences drive the demand for livestock products. Investors can access the livestock market through futures contracts, ETFs, or livestock-focused investment vehicles. Factors to consider include livestock production trends, feed costs, animal disease outbreaks, and consumer demand patterns.

Soft Commodities

Soft commodities, including coffee, cocoa, sugar, and cotton, possess distinctive characteristics and find various applications. Coffee and cocoa are consumed worldwide as popular beverages, sugar is a crucial sweetener, and cotton is used in the textile industry. Investors can gain exposure to soft commodities through futures contracts, ETFs, or commodity-focused mutual funds. Factors to consider include global supply and demand dynamics, weather conditions, disease outbreaks, and changing consumer preferences. Weather patterns, global supply disruptions, pest outbreaks, and sustainability concerns influence soft commodity prices. Environmental and social considerations in producing and sourcing soft commodities are increasingly important factors for investors to evaluate.

Structured Notes

What are Structured Notes

Structured notes are complex financial instruments that combine traditional investments, such as bonds or stocks, with derivative components. These hybrid securities expose investors to specific investment strategies or customized risk-return profiles. Financial institutions typically issue structured notes that can be tailored to meet the unique investment objectives of investors.

Structured notes derive value from an underlying asset or a combination of investments. These assets can include stocks, bonds, indices, commodities, currencies, or a combination thereof. The performance of the structured note is linked to the performance of the underlying asset(s).

Structured notes offer customization options, allowing investors to tailor the investment to their needs. Investors can choose various features, such as the underlying asset(s), maturity date, participation rate, and protection level. This customization allows investors to align the structured note with their risk appetite and investment objectives.

Structured notes are complex financial instruments that require a thorough understanding of their features and associated risks. They may involve a higher risk level than traditional investments, and investors should carefully assess the risks and potential rewards before investing. The complexity of structured notes also means they may be more suitable for experienced or sophisticated investors.

Angel Investing and Venture Capital

What is Angel Investing and Venture Capital?

Angel Investing and venture capital are very similar in that they both help start and support an entrepreneur with their startup.

Angel Investing

Angel investing is a private investment made by an often wealthy individual willing to take risks in hopes of receiving significant returns. Angel Investors are investing their money to finance the entrepreneur, taking on the risk. It's important to note that most startups fail, so it's essential that when the investors do well with a startup, they are making a profit. Angel Investors will usually fund startups when they start. This can be from the idea or when the company has a few thousand sales.

Angels source investment opportunities through various channels, including personal networks, angel groups, online platforms, and startup events. Diligent evaluation of potential investments involves assessing the team's capabilities, market potential, competitive landscape, and scalability. Angels negotiate investment terms, including valuation, ownership stake, liquidation preferences, and governance rights. Balancing the interests of the entrepreneur and the angel investor is crucial to establishing a mutually beneficial agreement.

Entrepreneur

49

Venture Capital

Another way startups are supported is through venture capital. Venture capital firms usually do not use their money to fund startups, so they take less risk. Although venture capital firms often put millions of dollars into startups, angel investors put up less. This happens because venture capital firms invest more money during the development phase and growth phase of the startup.

Venture capitalists, or VCs, actively seek investment opportunities through various channels, including referrals, entrepreneur networks, industry events, and pitch competitions. Rigorous screening processes are employed to evaluate the viability and potential of each startup. VCs conduct extensive due diligence, examining the market size, competitive landscape, team capabilities, intellectual property, and growth potential. This comprehensive analysis guides their investment decisions. VCs negotiate investment terms, including valuation, ownership percentage, board representation, and liquidation preferences. Balancing the interests of the entrepreneur and the VC is essential for establishing a mutually beneficial agreement.

Venture capitalists contribute significant value beyond financial investment. They provide mentorship, strategic guidance, and operational support to portfolio companies, leveraging their industry expertise and networks. VCs facilitate access to resources such as talent acquisition, business development opportunities, partnerships, and follow-on funding. Their networks and connections help startups navigate challenges and scale their operations.

Hedge Funds

What are Hedge Funds?

Hedge Funds are investment pools constantly managed by professionals who use multiple strategies to beat the market and generate higher returns for their customers/clients.

Hedge Funds use short selling, derivatives trading, and leverage. Short selling refers to the opposite of general investing because the investor makes a profit when the price of an asset goes down. Derivatives trading is when an individual buys and sells a contract derived from the value of an underlying asset such as stocks or oil. Finally, leverage is when funds are borrowed to increase the potential return on investment.

Since Hedge Funds are constantly managed, there are management and performance fees. Due to so many costs, wealthy investors often put their money into hedge funds and forget about it.

The biggest global hedge fund is Bridgewater Associates, which Ray Dalio founded. Bridgewater Associates manages $150 billion. Often you must have a net worth above $1 million to invest in Bridgewater.

Benefits of Hedge Funds

Hedge funds aim to deliver superior risk-adjusted returns by leveraging their expertise, market insights, and specialized strategies. The flexibility to take long and short positions allows them to capitalize on market inefficiencies and generate profits in various market conditions. Hedge funds provide access to non-traditional asset classes and investment strategies, which can enhance portfolio diversification.

By including hedge funds in an investment portfolio, investors can reduce their reliance on traditional asset classes such as stocks and bonds, potentially improving risk-adjusted returns. Hedge funds employ sophisticated risk management techniques to protect capital and mitigate downside risk. Using strategies such as hedging, short-selling, and arbitrage, hedge funds aim to generate positive returns while minimizing exposure to market volatility.

Risks and Considerations

Hedge funds often impose restrictions on investor liquidity, typically through lock-up periods and redemption restrictions. These limitations can make it challenging for investors to access their capital when needed, potentially impacting short-term liquidity requirements. Hedge funds employ complex investment strategies that may need help understanding fully. Additionally, they often provide limited transparency regarding portfolio holdings and trading activities. This lack of transparency can make it challenging for investors to assess the underlying risks and make informed investment decisions. Hedge funds generally have high minimum investment requirements, making them inaccessible to many individual investors. This exclusivity means that hedge funds are primarily accessible to accredited and institutional investors who meet specific wealth or income thresholds.

Brokers and Fiduciaries

What is a Broker?

Brokers act as intermediaries between buyers and sellers in the financial markets. They facilitate the execution of trades, enabling investors to buy and sell various securities, including stocks, bonds, options, and mutual funds. One of the primary advantages of working with brokers is their ease and convenience in executing transactions. By providing access to various exchanges and markets, brokers empower investors to participate in the vast world of investment opportunities.

Brokers offer a range of services and expertise that cater to the diverse needs of investors. These services can include investment research, market analysis, and access to proprietary trading platforms. By leveraging their knowledge and experience, brokers assist clients in making informed investment decisions. They provide valuable insights into market trends, company fundamentals, and macroeconomic factors that may impact investment performance. Furthermore, brokers often offer personalized advice tailored to individual investors' specific goals and risk tolerance.

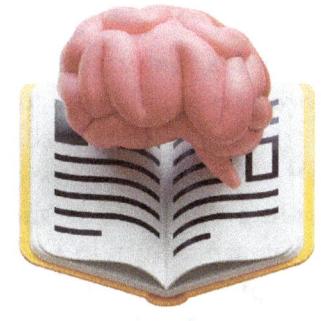

The financial industry is heavily regulated to protect investors' interests, and brokers are subject to specific regulations and oversight. In the United States, brokers are regulated by the Financial Industry Regulatory Authority (FINRA) and must adhere to specific rules and standards. These regulations aim to ensure fair dealing, transparency, and the suitability of investment recommendations.

What is a Fiduciary?

Fiduciaries hold a profound responsibility as stewards of their client's financial well-being. Unlike other financial professionals, fiduciaries are bound by a fiduciary duty, a legal and ethical obligation to act in their client's best interests. This duty requires the utmost care, loyalty, and prudence in managing clients' investments. Fiduciaries must place their client's interests above their own, avoiding any conflicts of interest that may compromise the integrity of their advice.

One of the primary advantages of working with a fiduciary is the comprehensive guidance and advice they offer. Fiduciaries go beyond simply executing trades; they engage in a holistic approach to investment management. By thoroughly understanding their client's financial objectives, risk tolerance, and time horizons, fiduciaries develop personalized investment strategies tailored to each client's unique circumstances.

Fiduciaries conduct in-depth research, perform rigorous due diligence, and consider various investment options to construct well-diversified portfolios aligned with their client's goals. They continuously monitor and evaluate investment performance, making adjustments when necessary. Fiduciaries act as educators, providing clients with the knowledge and understanding they need to make informed investment decisions.

Transparency and disclosure are core principles for fiduciaries. They strive to provide clear and comprehensive information about fees, potential conflicts of interest, and the rationale behind their investment recommendations. By maintaining open lines of communication, fiduciaries empower their clients to make informed choices and understand the implications of their investment decisions.

Option Trading

What is Option Trading?

Options Trading involves the buying and selling of options contracts. An option is an agreement between two parties that gives the buyer the right, but not the obligation, to buy or sell an underlying asset at a predetermined price and time in the future.

A call option is a contract used in options trading that lets the buyer buy the underlying asset at a fixed or strike price on or before a particular date. This indicates that the buyer has the choice, but it is optional to purchase the asset. On the other hand, a put option is a contract that enables the buyer to sell the underlying asset at a predetermined price on or before a given date. This indicates that the buyer has the choice but is not required to sell the item. Investors use both calls and put options to control risk, predict future market movements, or make money by selling options contracts.

Benefits of Option Trading

Options trading offers the potential for amplified returns through leverage. Options allow investors to control a more significant amount of an underlying asset with a smaller initial investment, thereby magnifying potential gains compared to traditional investments. Options serve as practical tools for risk management and hedging. This investment can be utilized to protect a portfolio against downside risk, manage exposure to volatile markets, and enhance overall risk-adjusted returns. Option trading provides flexibility and versatility in adapting to different market conditions. Options can be employed for income generation, speculation, capital preservation, and other investment objectives. Finally this investment allow investors to design strategies that align with their specific market outlook and risk tolerance.

Risks and Considerations

Options have finite lifespans, and their value is influenced by time decay. Time decay and understanding the impact of time remaining until expiration on option prices and trading decisions is vital for investing. Options trading involves complex ideas and strategies. Thorough understanding, education, and continuous learning are essential for making financial gains. Investors should conduct thorough research, utilize educational resources, and practice simulated trading to gain familiarity and confidence in options trading.

Forex Trading

What is Forex Trading?

Forex Trading, or foreign exchange trading, involves buying and selling currencies in the foreign exchange market. If you have ever gone to a foreign country and had to exchange money, you have already participated in forex trading.

Forex trading has been known to be volatile and risky, but it can also provide high returns. Investors can make money consistently because the market is open for 24 hours. Investments can be short, similar to day trading, but sometimes assets can last for months. The ultimate goal of forex trading is to make a profit from fluctuating currency prices.

- - - - - - - - - - - - - - - - - - -

Forex Trading is a market that requires a deep understanding of market research, risk management, and trading strategies because it is extremely liquid, volatile, and offers huge chances for wins and losses. Several financial products, such as currency pairs, futures contracts, options, and exchange-traded funds, are used in forex trading (ETFs).

Benefits of Forex Trading

The forex market is the most liquid financial market globally, with high trading volumes and tight bid-ask spreads. Liquidity and accessibility provide ample trading opportunities, allowing investors to enter and exit positions efficiently. Forex trading offers high leverage, enabling traders to control more prominent positions with a relatively small initial investment. The potential for magnified returns that influence provides and the associated risks comes with Forex trading. Furthermore, Forex trading allows investors to diversify their portfolios by adding currencies to their asset mix. Forex instruments can serve as practical hedging tools to manage currency risk in international investments.

Risks and Considerations

The forex market is characterized by volatility, presenting both opportunities and risks. It's important to consider the importance of risk management techniques, such as setting stop-loss orders, managing position sizes, and avoiding excessive leverage to mitigate potential losses. Forex trading involves analyzing both fundamental factors and technical indicators. Its essential to understand how fundamental analysis considers economic data, news events, and central bank policies, while technical analysis utilizes charts, patterns, and hands to make trading decisions. Successful forex trading requires emotional discipline and a solid understanding of trading psychology. The psychological challenges traders face, such as fear, greed, and overtrading play a role in the profits made when trading.

Forex Trading Strategies

Trend-following strategies, such as moving averages, trendlines, and breakout trading, aim to profit from sustained price movements in a particular direction. Range trading strategies capitalize on price fluctuations within defined support and resistance levels. Techniques include support and resistance zones, Bollinger Bands, and oscillators for identifying and trading range-bound markets. Carry trade strategies involve capitalizing on interest rate differentials between currencies, while news trading focuses on trading currency pairs based on significant news releases and their impact on exchange rates.

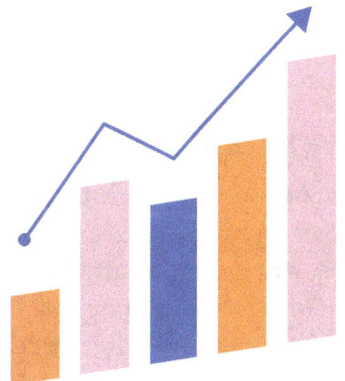

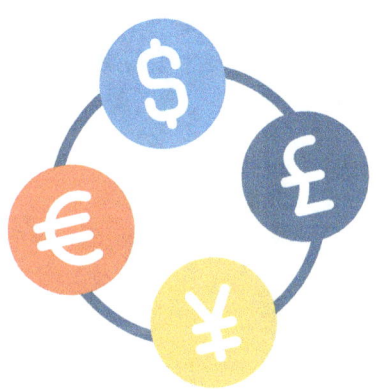

The forex market is the largest financial market in the world, with an average daily trading volume of around $6.6 trillion. This is significantly higher than the combined trading volume of all the world's stock markets. The vast size and liquidity of the forex market make it an attractive playground for traders looking for ample trading opportunities and quick execution of trades.

Forex trading offers immense potential for investors to profit from the global currency market. By understanding the fundamentals, risks, and strategies of forex trading, investors can confidently navigate the market and make informed trading decisions. Continuous learning, disciplined risk management, and a resilient mindset are vital for long-term success in forex trading.

ESG Investing

What is ESG Investing

Environmental, Social, and Governance or ESG investing incorporates environmental, social, and governance factors into investment analysis and decision-making processes. The historical development of ESG investing, from ethical and socially responsible investing to the more comprehensive framework of ESG integration is crucial to comprehend.

Critical components of ESG investing include various ESG factors and metrics. Environmental factors include climate change, resource usage, pollution, and biodiversity. Social factors encompass human rights, labor practices, community engagement, and diversity. Governance factors include board composition, executive compensation, shareholder rights, and transparency. Understanding these factors is necessary for evaluating companies' sustainability and societal impact.

ESG Investment Strategies

Investors can incorporate ESG factors into their portfolio construction process. This involves integrating ESG data and analysis alongside traditional financial analysis, ensuring that investments align with economic and ESG objectives. Impact investing aims to generate positive, measurable social and environmental impacts alongside financial returns. It can contribute to achieving the United Nations' Sustainable Development Goals (SDGs). Active ownership involves exercising shareholder rights and engaging with companies on ESG issues. Proxy voting, dialogue with company management, and collaboration with other investors can drive positive change.

Alternative Investments

What are Alternative Investments?

Alternative investments are any other investment that isn't traditionally seen as an investment. Almost anything can be an investment if you think that the investment will go up or down in value. Some examples of alternative investments are art, cars, wine, books, sports cards, and more.

Often alternative investments can provide great value and many benefits as well. Take art, for example; art can rise in value and is often bought for millions of dollars. Not only that, but sometimes buying art can help with tax right offs, which ultimately help the investor save money.

Sometimes alternative investments can be less liquid. On top of this, researching is also crucial because it isn't guaranteed that the things you purchase will gain in value.

Trading cards have recently been an investment to consider for many sports fans as these pieces of cardboard can go for lots of money—a 1952 Mickey Mantle baseball card sold for $12.6 million, which was the most expensive selling ever. Trading cards for all sports are not that expensive, and many ranges from just $1-$2, but many go into the thousands. From basketball to football, there is a sport for many cards and an opportunity for investors to cash in.

61

Famous Investors

Warren Buffett

Warren Buffett is an American investor, corporate tycoon, and philanthropist. Warren is the head chairman and CEO of Berkshire Hathaway. Berkshire Hathaway owns and runs various businesses for insurance, real estate, manufacturing, etc. With a net worth of over $100 billion, Buffett is usually regarded as one of the most successful investors in history. He is renowned for his value investing strategy, which entails purchasing assets below their intrinsic value and holding them for an extended period. Buffett has promised to donate the majority of his riches to philanthropic causes. He has won numerous honors for his professional and charitable accomplishments, and Time Magazine has named him one of the world's most influential people.

Carl Icahn

Carl Icahn is an American businessman and investor. Icahn founded Icahn Enterprises, which runs investment, energy, automotive, and much more businesses. Icahn is renowned for his activist investment strategy, which entails buying substantial corporate stakes and using his clout to demand adjustments to management or business practices to boost shareholder value. One of the most successful investors in history, Icahn has a net worth of more than $20 billion. He is also a well-known philanthropist who has given millions of dollars to organizations such as Mount Sinai and the Children's Rescue Fund.

Charles Schwab

Charles Schwab is an American investor, businessman, and philanthropist. He is the founder and former CEO of the Charles Schwab Company, a brokerage firm that provides individual investors and institutions with various investing and financial services. He is also well-known for donating millions to charities supporting the arts and education. He is regarded as one of the most influential figures in finance and has a net worth of more than $14 billion.

John Templeton

John Templeton was an American-British businessman and investor. He founded the John Templeton Foundation, which provides funding for humanities and social sciences studies. He was a devoted philanthropist who gave millions of dollars to causes like education and medical research. He won many awards for his services to the charitable and investment worlds. At age 95, John Templeton passed away in 2008, leaving behind a legacy as a trailblazing philanthropist and investor across the globe.

Bill Ackman

American investor, hedge fund manager, and philanthropist Bill Ackman is the founder and CEO of Pershing Square Capital Management. This activist hedge fund has made some high-profile investments. He has taken part in several important investments, such as a profitable wager against the subprime mortgage market in the middle of the 2000s and a prominent investment in the pharmaceutical business Valeant. He has won multiple honors for his contributions to the investment sector and has been named one of the most influential individuals in finance by Forbes magazine.

John C. Bogle

American investor, entrepreneur, and philanthropist John C. Bogle is best known for helping to start the Vanguard Group, one of the biggest mutual fund companies in the world. Bogle was a pioneer in the index fund sector, and in 1976 he introduced the first index fund, which completely changed how investors thought about the stock market. He received various honors throughout his career, including the Presidential Medal of Freedom, and is regarded as one of the most significant figures in financial history. At 89, Bogle passed away in 2019, leaving behind a legacy as a relentless supporter of small investors and a proponent of honest and open trading.

How Can YOU Get Started?

Now that you know there are so many options to build your wealth and be financially stable through investing, it's time to take action. Before splurging your money on investments, it's essential that you take into consideration many things. First, you want to assess your financial situation. You think about your income, expenses, debt, and savings. It's crucial that when investing, you have a budget and plan out saying how much you will support every month, year, etc. You need to understand that you might not be able to invest much right now, but it's essential that you get started with a little bit and build the habits of investing regularly.

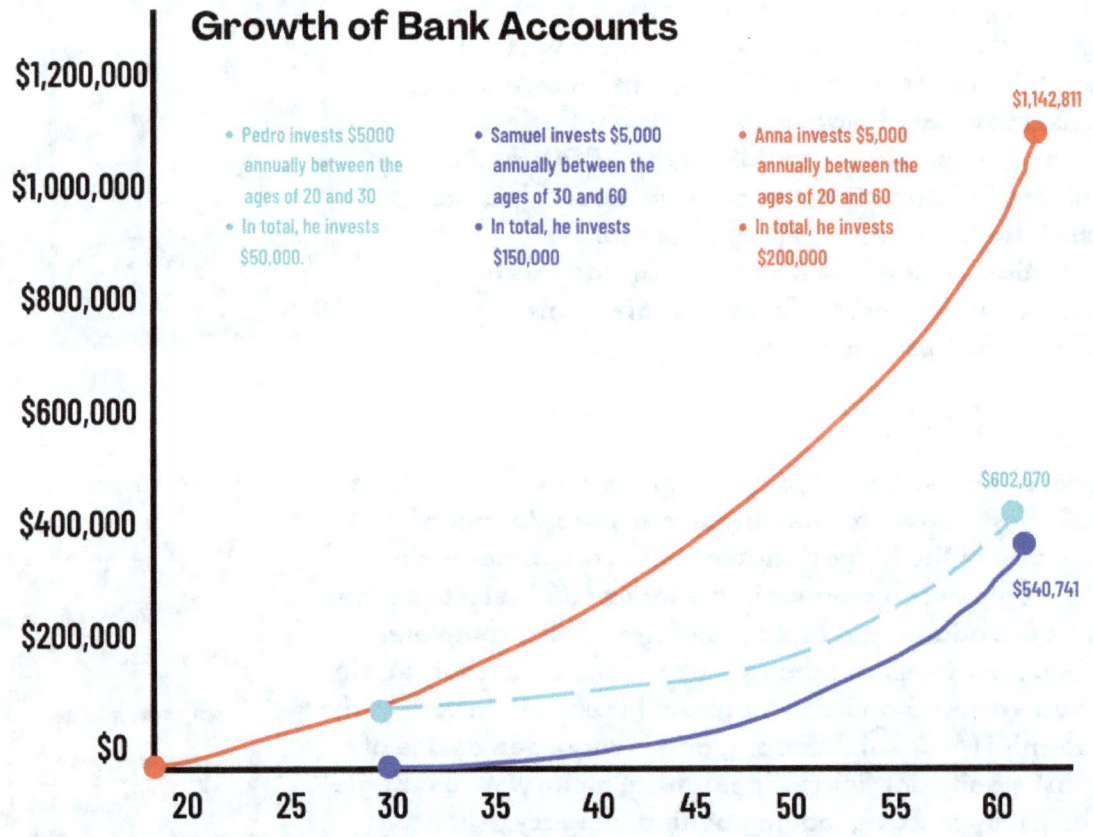

Growth of Bank Accounts

- Pedro invests $5000 annually between the ages of 20 and 30
- In total, he invests $50,000.

- Samuel invests $5,000 annually between the ages of 30 and 60
- In total, he invests $150,000

- Anna invests $5,000 annually between the ages of 20 and 60
- In total, he invests $200,000

$1,142,811

$602,070

$540,741

This graph shows that by investing earlier and being consistent for an extended period, you can make upwards of $500,000+ by the time you retire.

It is also essential to consider your goals when it comes to investing. Are you investing to be a millionaire, to save money for a home, to retire, etc? This can impact how risky and what types of investments will be best for you because an investment portfolio should be unique to your own financial goals that you want to achieve.

I think a significant consideration is your risk tolerance. Do you want to put your money in more volatile markets and risk losing a substantial portion with the upside of winning big? Now, this will depend on your personality, age, background, value, goals, etc., but it's crucial that you assess the risks and plan out how risky or safe your investments will be.

It will also be crucial to further educate yourself on topics like the one explained in this introductory book, as only the basics were covered. This book is intended to make the towering idea of investing accessible for individuals who are not experts and be able to pick up this short book and spark their journey into being intelligent investors. The basic is a great place to start, but by taking it to the next level and doing independent research, you can get to the next level and ensure control of your future.

Many people can get started with a 401k with their employer or a (Roth) IRA, as these are the most common investment markets for people. Many jobs already offer these plans, so it's essential that you take advantage of them.

You must open a custodial account for people under 18 years old/ as you can wait to own a personal investment account. This account will have more limitations than a regular investment account, but it's better to start now with investing, even if it's just a few dollars.

Sources

"Bill Ackman." Wikipedia. Wikimedia Foundation, March 18, 2023. https://en.wikipedia.org/wiki/Bill_Ackman.

"Carl Icahn." Wikipedia. Wikimedia Foundation, February 19, 2023. https://en.wikipedia.org/wiki/Carl_Icahn.

"Charles R. Schwab." Wikipedia. Wikimedia Foundation, March 17, 2023. https://en.wikipedia.org/wiki/Charles_R._Schwab.

"Cryptocurrency Exchange for Bitcoin, Ethereum & Altcoins." Binance. Accessed March 18, 2023. https://www.binance.com/en.

Investopedia. Investopedia. Accessed March 18, 2023. https://www.investopedia.com/.

"John C. Bogle." Wikipedia. Wikimedia Foundation, February 14, 2023. https://en.wikipedia.org/wiki/John_C._Bogle.

"John Templeton." Wikipedia. Wikimedia Foundation, January 26, 2023. https://en.wikipedia.org/wiki/John_Templeton.

ROBBINS, TONY. Money: Master the Game. SIMON & SCHUSTER LTD, 2017.

Tyson, Eric. Investing for Dummies. Hoboken, NJ: John Wiley & Sons, Inc., 2021.

"Warren Buffett." Wikipedia. Wikimedia Foundation, March 11, 2023. https://en.wikipedia.org/wiki/Warren_Buffett.

"Yahoo Finance - Stock Market Live, Quotes, Business & Finance News." Yahoo! Finance. Yahoo! Accessed March 18, 2023. https://finance.yahoo.com/.

www.ingramcontent.com/pod-product-compliance
Lightning Source LLC
Chambersburg PA
CBHW082148290526
45794CB00008B/3215